HISTORY OF FUN STUFF

The Tricks and Treats of Halloween!

by Angela Murphy

illustrated by Rich Wake

Ready-to-Read

Simon Spotlight
New York London Toronto Sydney New Delhi

SIMON SPOTLIGHT
An imprint of Simon & Schuster Children's Publishing Division
1230 Avenue of the Americas, New York, New York 10020
This Simon Spotlight edition August 2014
Text copyright © 2014 by Simon & Schuster, Inc.
Illustrations copyright © 2014 by Rich Wake
All rights reserved, including the right of reproduction in whole or in part in any form.
SIMON SPOTLIGHT, READY-TO-READ, and colophon are registered trademarks
of Simon & Schuster, Inc.
For information about special discounts for bulk purchases, please contact Simon & Schuster Special Sales at
1-866-506-1949 or business@simonandschuster.com.
Manufactured in China 0915 SDI

CONTENTS

CHAPTER 1
How Did It Begin?

If you think really hard, you can probably come up with some facts you already know about Halloween. For example, you know that Halloween falls on October 31 every year in the United States, right? And you almost definitely know that most kids like to go trick-or-treating and get loaded up with candy on Halloween, don't you?

So, you already know a thing or two about Halloween. But do you know how it began? Or why people dress up in costumes to go trick-or-treating? Or how carving pumpkins became a part of the holiday?

By the time you finish reading this book, you will know the answers to those questions, and many more! You will be a History of Fun Stuff Expert on Halloween!

Many people believe that Halloween has its origins in Europe in the ancient Celtic [KEL-tik] festival of Samhain [SOW-in]. This festival, which took place every year on November 1, celebrated the end of summer and the beginning of winter. The Celts would wear costumes and have ceremonies to protect their crops from spirits.

They believed that the spirits might come damage their crops and that the costumes would scare the spirits away. The costumes and the spooky spirits sound a little bit similar to modern Halloween, don't they?

Another ancient people, the Romans, had day-long festivals to celebrate the harvest and to honor those who had died. One of these was a day for Pomona, the goddess of fruit and orchards. They also had a day to honor the dead, called Feralia.

The Romans are famous for their vast empire. At its largest, it went as far north

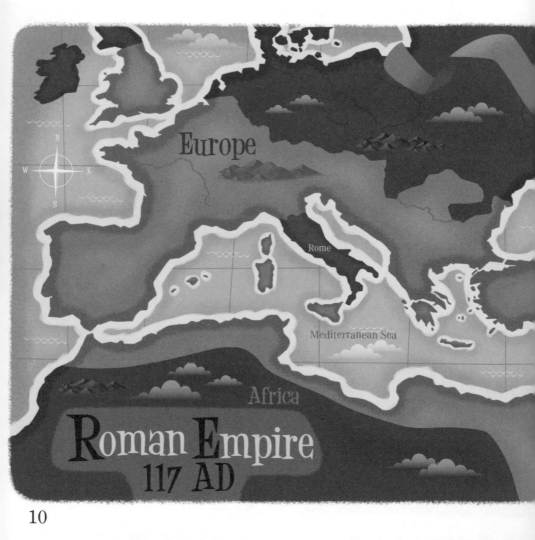

Europe

Rome

Mediterranean Sea

Africa

Roman Empire
117 AD

as England, and as far south as Egypt. It also stretched west to Spain and east to today's Middle East. By 43 AD, the Romans had conquered the territories of the Celts in England, and over the next few centuries, some of the customs from their Pomona and Feralia festivals merged with those of Samhain.

Halloween has also been closely linked to a Christian holiday called All Saints' Day, or All Hallows' Day, which comes much later in history than Samhain and continues to be celebrated today. Like Samhain, All Saints' Day occurs on November 1. The night before is called All Hallows' Eve, which eventually became known as Halloween.

Throughout the centuries, people have celebrated All Saints' Day in many ways, including dressing up like devils, angels, and saints, and marching in parades to honor Christian saints. The costumes and parades sound a little similar to modern Halloween too, right?

As time went on, traditions changed. Halloween lost some of its religious meaning and instead became a holiday that was meant to bring people together for fun and celebration. In the United States, it is estimated that Americans spend eight billion dollars on Halloween every year! Halloween is the second largest commercial

holiday that is celebrated. Can you guess what the *most* popular one is? (Here's a hint: Think of a guy with a big white beard who dresses up in a red suit and lives in the North Pole.) If you guessed Christmas, you are correct! And speaking of dressing up, one of the most fun things about Halloween is choosing your costume!

CHAPTER 2
Finding the Perfect Costume

Back in the early days of Halloween, people assigned a lot of meaning to their Halloween costumes. Remember the costumes people wore on All Saints' Day? In modern times, the sky is the limit when it comes to Halloween costumes! Some people love to dress up in spooky costumes, like ghosts or vampires, while other people love to dress up as sports players, movie stars, or famous historical figures. Some people even dress up as characters from a favorite book or television show. If you can think of it, you can probably dress up as it for Halloween!

No one knows for sure what the most popular Halloween costume is throughout the ages, but there are some very popular options that have been around for a long time, like witches, black cats, skeletons, Frankenstein's monster, and ghosts. Have you ever dressed up in one of those classic costumes?

Nowadays Halloween costumes can be purchased or rented, or they can be made at home. Some fun homemade Halloween costumes we've heard about include a bag of jelly beans, a tree, and a giant meatball!

What is the silliest homemade costume you can think of? Whatever costume you choose, one thing is for sure: Costumes are a fun part of one of Halloween's most beloved traditions—trick-or-treating!

CHAPTER 3
Trick . . . or Treat?

Trick-or-treating seems to have grown out of a variety of traditions that have been observed through the centuries. Remember the festival of Samhain and the spirits the Celts wanted to protect their crops from? Well, it turns out the Celts would not only dress up in costumes to keep the spirits away, thereby "tricking" them, but they would also put out treats for the spirits to keep them happy.

Later, as All Saints' Day grew in popularity, another tradition took hold in England: making soul cakes. Soul cakes were biscuits that were handed out to the poor, or to performers who traveled from town to town. As time went on, the tradition changed and children began to go around to different houses in search of cakes or little presents.

Meanwhile, in Scotland and Ireland, another tradition was evolving. It was called "guising," related to the word "disguise." Children would dress up and go from door to door, performing "tricks," like singing, telling jokes or stories, or other displays of talents. For their efforts, the people who lived in the houses would give out treats, like fruit, nuts, or coins.

Speaking of traveling, as you know, Halloween eventually came to the United States, but it didn't happen overnight. With the exception of some southern states, Halloween wasn't widely celebrated in the United States until the middle of the 1800s. However when it was first celebrated, it was more like a harvest festival than today's holiday.

By the second half of the 1800s, more immigrants began arriving. Many of them came from Ireland. Ireland was going through a time of hardship called the Great Potato Famine, and immigrants came to the United States in search of a better life. They brought many of their Halloween customs with them, and Halloween began to grow more and more popular and resemble what we know and love about Halloween today.

By the early 1900s, Halloween had taken a firm hold in the United States. Entire towns celebrated with parades and parties, but it wasn't all fun and games. There was a dark side to Halloween. Some people were going too far and damaging property. In order to put a stop to this, townspeople shifted the focus of the holiday to children, and trick-or-treating as we know it was born. By the 1950s, trick-or-treating had become the focus of Halloween. And what is the best part of trick-or-treating? Candy, of course!

Today, giving out candy is as much a part of Halloween as giving out valentines on Valentine's Day. Remember the eight billion dollars spent on Halloween? Well, one quarter of that, or two billion dollars, is spent just on candy alone! What kind of candy is your favorite?

What about candy corn? Love it or hate it, Americans sure do eat a lot of it. Thirty-five million pounds of candy corn are eaten each year! That's nine billion pieces! There's even a National Candy Corn Day on October 30, the day before Halloween.

Candy corn was invented in 1880 by a man in Philadelphia named George Renninger. But it wasn't called candy corn back then. It was known as chicken feed. Doesn't sound quite as appealing, does it?

Another Halloween treat is the age-old practice of bobbing for apples. Now merely a fun party game where you have to grab an apple with your teeth without using your hands, it was once part of a tradition of fortune-telling that would be done around Halloween. It was believed that the first person who successfully got an apple during a round of the game would be the first one to be married. That's a lot of pressure on one little apple!

CHAPTER 4
Spooky Symbols

What would Halloween be without decorations to help set the spooky mood? For one thing, it wouldn't be as colorful. October is ruled by orange and black. Why orange? For the harvest and pumpkins, of course! During the month of October, you probably see lots of pumpkins and pumpkin-themed Halloween decorations all around. But did you know that pumpkins are native to the Americas and that, like tomatoes, they are fruits, not vegetables?

The heaviest pumpkin on record weighed more than two thousand pounds. To put that in perspective, imagine the size of an average crocodile. Now imagine two crocodiles. That's about how much that pumpkin weighed!

But Halloween isn't just about pumpkins, it's also about carving them.

The first jack-o'-lanterns made in England and Ireland centuries ago were created by carving turnips, potatoes, and even beets. It wasn't until Halloween started being celebrated in the United States, and people discovered that pumpkins were bigger and easier to carve, that they became the go-to fruit for jack-o'-lanterns. But how did carving fruits and vegetables become a tradition in the first place? It comes from an old Irish legend about a trickster named Stingy Jack. As punishment for his pranks, Jack was forced to wander from place to place with only a lantern made from a hollowed-out turnip as his guide.

Originally, Stingy Jack was also known as Jack of the Lantern, but over the decades, that was shortened to Jack O' Lantern.

The other color associated with Halloween is black. Black symbolizes the night sky and black cats. But how did these furry felines end up becoming a staple of Halloween decorations?

A long time ago, people believed black cats were associated with dark magic, and

through the years, they were added to the
assortment of Halloween symbols. These
days we know that black cats are just like
any other cats, sweet and adorable. And
we also know something else about them:
Dressing up like one makes for a great and
easy Halloween costume!

HISTORY
OF FUN STUFF
EXPERT
ON
HALLOWEEN

EXPERT

Congratulations! You've come to the end of this book. You are now an official History of Fun Stuff Expert on Halloween. Go ahead and impress your friends and family with all the cool things you know about the spookiest night of the year! And when it's time to go trick-or-treating, remember everything you've learned about the many traditions that led up to Halloween, and enjoy!

Hey, kids! Now that you're an expert on the history of Halloween, turn the page to learn even more about it, and some geography, science, and trivia along the way!

Festivals Around the World

In America we celebrate Halloween every October. Check out these similar holidays that are celebrated around the world!

Italy – Carnevale – February/March – About six weeks prior to Easter, before the beginning of Lent  (a time of fasting), Catholic people in Italy and many other countries around the world hold a celebration called *Carnevale* or "Carnival." People dress up in bright costumes and wear ornately decorated masks while attending big parties and lively parades.

England – Guy Fawkes Day – November 5th – On this day in 1605, soldiers thwarted a plot against King James I. The English celebrate this national day of thanks with bonfires, fireworks, and parades.

Mexico – El Dia de los Muertos – November 1st –  **November 2nd –** "The Day of the Dead" is a special time for people to remember their loved ones who have died. They build an altar in their home to their relatives who have passed away, attend colorful parades in honor of the dead, and later gather at the graveyard for a picnic.

India – Kali Puja – October/November – In India, many Hindu people celebrate the triumph of good over evil during the festival of Kali Puja. They stay up until dawn singing, lighting candles, doing magic tricks, and setting off fireworks in honor of the goddess Kali.

China – Yu Lan – August/September – "The Festival of the Hungry Ghosts" is believed to be the one time of the year when spirits roam the world. People burn pictures of money or food as offerings to the spirit world and to satisfy the ghosts.

Japan – The Obon Festival – July/August – The Japanese dedicate this Buddhist festival to the spirits of their ancestors. Special foods are prepared, and people light red lanterns to guide their lost loved ones home.

How Do Pumpkins Grow?

Pumpkins are the stars of October, but what's happening to those pumpkins during the other eleven months of the year? Check out the life cycle of a pumpkin below!

Seed – Pumpkin seeds are planted and watered in late May. If the seed is healthy and has a good environment to grow in, the seed will become a . . .

Seedling – The seed keeps growing, sprouting up and through the soil. The plant also grows its roots deeper into the ground so that it can absorb more nutrients from the soil and grow into a . . .

Vine – The plant spreads up and out, growing big leaves and tendrils called vines. Now the pumpkin plant is ready to . . .

Flower – The plant soon grows a big yellow flower, which means that it is ready to produce a baby pumpkin. The flower soon makes a . . .

Fruit – The flower falls away to reveal a baby pumpkin! The pumpkin is green at first, but turns orange as it develops. Pumpkins are important to the life cycle of the plant because they carry . . .

New Seeds – With winter approaching, the old pumpkin plant dies. As the days get colder and the pumpkin itself decays, the seeds ooze out of it, allowing a new plant to be born the following spring. You might recognize these same seeds from when you carved out your jack-o'-lantern!

Animals of Halloween

Black cats, spiders, and bats have been the unofficial mascots of Halloween for years. Check out these facts about Halloween's most popular animals below!

Black Cats

- Ancient Egyptians believed that black cats were extremely lucky.
- Black fur color is a common trait in cats, and so many cats have black fur.
- King Charles I of England was said to own a black cat, which he considered to be good luck. He kept the cat under constant, close guard at the palace.

Spiders

- Spiders are not insects; they are arachnids. Other arachnids include scorpions, mites, and ticks.
- Spiders eat more bugs than birds and bats combined. Talk about great insect repellant!
- Most spiders only live for a year, but some tarantulas have life spans of twenty-five years or longer!

Bats

- Bats are the only mammals (warm-blooded animals with fur) that can fly.
- Bats see in the dark using sound waves—much like how submarines use sonar to see underwater!
- Bats hang upside down when they roost, wrapping their wings around themselves to keep warm.

Being an expert on something means you can get an awesome score on a quiz on that subject! Take this

HISTORY OF HALLOWEEN QUIZ

to see how much you've learned.

1. The ancient Celtic festival of _____ celebrated the end of summer and the beginning of winter.

a. Samhain   b. Feralia   c. All Saints' Day

2. Which empire conquered the Celts in 43 AD?

a. Persian   b. Roman   c. Chinese

3. "Halloween" got its name from _____, the night before All Saints' Day.

a. Pomona   b. Bonfire Night   c. All Hallows' Eve

4. In Scotland and Ireland, children would go "guising," performing tricks in return for what?

a. Smelly socks   b. Treats   c. Jack-o'-lanterns

5. In the United States, when did trick-or-treating become the main focus of Halloween?

a. 12th century AD   b. 1950s   c. Mid 1800s

6. Many Irish immigrants came to America in the late 1800s because of the_____.

a. Great Potato Famine   b. Meatball Conundrum   c. First World War

7. The first jack-o'-lanterns were carved out of turnips, potatoes, and even _____.

a. Wood   b. Beets   c. Cucumbers

8. Which of these Halloweenlike celebrations honor the memory of those who have died?

a. Carnevale and Kali Puja   b. Halloween   c. El Dia de los Muertos, Yu Lan, and the Obon Festival

Answers: 1.a 2.b 3.c 4.b 5.b 6.a 7.b 8.c